A Hemingway Check List

LEE SAMUELS

Charles Scribner's Sons

NEW YORK · 1951

PRINTED IN THE UNITED STATES OF AMERICA

Preface

LEE SAMUELS is a man, who, with no wish to profit from it, finds and collects all that you have written and then lost or forgotten. He not only finds them. He gives you copies of them for better or for worse. Finally they are to be given to a library. It is such a disinterested action that it is impressive to the point of being almost incredible in these times.

It is too easy to remember sending a story to a limited edition publisher (payment nil) and asking the return of the manuscript as it was the only copy you had. A few years later you were asked to authenticate the manuscript (which was accompanied by a letter requesting its return), in a Chicago book-store where you had gone to buy something to read on the train.

That was the most disabusing transaction except for the constant theft of any first editions from the house by uninvited guests and by the guests of people to whom one had loaned the house. The first of the early first editions was small and fitted easily into a guest's pocket. There was another that was a little large. But not too large to slip under a guest's coat.

Then there was the problem of the disposal of what you have written by people one lives with.

The simplest way to dispose of anything in a periodical is to have the periodical thrown away in the interests of house-keeping. This reached its climax in a town called Key West, Florida. The disposal of manuscripts was ably accomplished by taking them out of your filing cabinets and putting them in cardboard boxes where they were eaten by mice, rats and roaches. This, with the aid of the climate, was almost infallible. It was as successful in destruction as the incinerator and it made no smoke nor ashes. Poems also disappeared without a trace. They are still missing.

There were always other ways of disposing of what the man a woman is married to writes including the loss of everything the husband had written and not yet published (original manuscript, typewritten copy and carbons; each in its separate folder) through having a suitcase stolen in the Gare de Lyons in 1922. A man's wife was bringing the manuscript and carbons for him to work on during a Christmas Vacation from working for The Toronto Star, INS and Universal Service at the Lausanne conference. The suitcase was stolen while she went out to buy herself a bottle of Vittel water.

But you do not marry a woman for her ability to care for manuscripts and I truly felt sorrier for how awfully she felt than I did for the loss of everything I had written. She was a lovely and loyal woman with bad luck with manuscripts. Anyway one story was not lost. It was called "My Old Man" and Lincoln Steffens had sent it out to a magazine from which it was duly returned. It thus became my literary capital. We used to call it "Das Kapital."

Of course Lee cannot find these things that were lost; and I have lost plenty myself: unassisted. But he has shown that he can find anything existent for whatever use it may have. I wish to thank him for his inexhaustible patience and for his kindness.

ERNEST HEMINGWAY
Finca Vigia
San Francisco de Paula
Cuba, 11/8/50

The Books

THREE STORIES AND TEN POEMS

was published by the Contact Publishing Co., Paris, summer of 1923 in an edition of 300 copies. The three stories, UP IN MICHIGAN, OUT OF SEASON and MY OLD MAN appeared here for the first time. Of the ten poems, OKLAHOMA, CAPTIVES, MONTPARNASSE and ALONG WITH YOUTH were previously unpublished. Under the title "WANDERINGS," the following six poems appeared in Poetry, A Magazine of Verse, Chicago, January, 1923: MITRAILIATRICE, OILY WEATHER, ROOSEVELT, RIPARTO D'ASSALTO, CHAMPS D'HONNEUR and CHAPTER HEADING.

in our time

170 copies were printed at the three mountains press, Paris, in the spring of 1924. The first six chapters (of the eighteen) appeared in the Exiles No. of the Little Review, Paris, Spring, 1923. Three of the chapters were titled in the New York edition of IN OUR TIME as follows: Chapter 10, A VERY SHORT STORY, Chapter 11, THE REVOLUTIONIST, Chapter 18, L'ENVOI.

IN OUR TIME

Published by Boni and Liveright, New York, September 15, 1925 in an edition of 1335 copies. Four stories, THE END OF SOMETHING, THE THREE DAY BLOW, THE BATTLER and CAT IN THE RAIN appeared here for the first time. The remaining eleven stories had been published previously, as had the preface and the chapters indicated only by Roman numerals.

THE TORRENTS OF SPRING

Published by Charles Scribner's Sons, New York, on May 28, 1926 in a first printing of 1250 copies.

TODAY IS FRIDAY

This little pamphlet was published in an edition of 300 copies (of which 260 were for sale) as an As Stable Publication in Englewood, N. J., summer of 1926.

THE SUN ALSO RISES

The publisher was Scribners, the date October 22, 1926 and there were 5090 copies of the first edition.

MEN WITHOUT WOMEN

Published by Scribners in a first printing of 7650 copies on October 14, 1927. This book contained 14 stories of which ten had been published previously. The four new stories were: A SIMPLE ENQUIRY, TEN INDIANS, A PURSUIT RACE and NOW I LAY ME.

A FAREWELL TO ARMS

was first published as a serial in Scribner's Magazine and ran from May to October, 1929. It appeared in book form on September 27, 1929 in a regular trade edition of 31,000 copies, plus a large paper, limited edition of 510 copies. The second issue of the first (trade) edition contains a short, author's note on p. (x).

IN OUR TIME

Published by Scribners on October 24, 1930—3000 copies. The only new material in this edition is the introduction, which appeared as ON THE QUAI AT SMYRNA in THE FIFTH COLUMN AND THE FIRST FORTY-NINE STORIES.

DEATH IN THE AFTERNOON

was published by Scribners in a first printing of 10,300 copies on September 23, 1932.

GOD REST YOU MERRY GENTLEMEN

a short story, was published separately by the House of Books, Ltd., New York, 1933. This was a limited edition of 300 copies.

WINNER TAKE NOTHING

This collection of fourteen short stories was published by Scribner's on October 27, 1933. There were 20,300 copies. The following seven stories appeared here for the first time: THE LIGHT OF THE WORLD, A WAY YOU'LL NEVER BE, THE MOTHER OF A QUEEN, ONE READER WRITES, A DAY'S WAIT, A NATURAL HISTORY OF THE DEAD, THE GAMBLER, THE NUN AND THE RADIO, and FATHERS AND SONS. The remaining stories had been previously published.

THE GREEN HILLS OF AFRICA

was published as a serial in Scribner's Magazine, running from May through November, 1935. In book form, there were 10,550 copies also published by Scribners—October 25, 1935. Edward Shenton did the decorations.

TO HAVE AND HAVE NOT

Scribners published 10,130 copies of this novel on October 15, 1937. Part I appeared in Cosmopolitan magazine in the April, 1934 issue. It was entitled ONE TRIP ACROSS and Rockwell Kent did some illustrations for it.

THE SPANISH EARTH

was published by the J. B. Savage Co., Cleveland, in June, 1938. There were 1000 numbered copies. Also contained herein was THE HEAT AND THE COLD which was reprinted from Verve magazine.

THE FIFTH COLUMN AND THE FIRST FORTY-NINE STORIES

was published by Scribners on October 14, 1938. There were 5350 copies. THE FIFTH COLUMN, a play, was hitherto unpublished. This was the first appearance in book form of four of the stories: THE SHORT HAPPY LIFE OF FRANCIS MACOMBER, THE CAPITAL OF THE WORLD (which was published as THE HORNS OF THE BULL in Esquire, June, 1936), THE SNOWS OF KILIMANJARO and OLD MAN AT THE BRIDGE.

FOR WHOM THE BELL TOLLS

Published by Scribners on October 21, 1940, the first edition consisted of 75,000 copies.

A FAREWELL TO ARMS

This illustrated (by Daniel Rasmusson) edition of 5300 copies was published on November 15, 1948 by Scribners. It contains a new introduction (dated June 30, 1948, Finca Vigia, San Francisco de Paula, Cuba) by the author.

FOR WHOM THE BELL TOLLS

Although this edition contains no new material, it is included for various reasons. It was published by The Limited Editions Club, New York, October, 1942. There were 1500 copies signed by the artist, Lynd Ward, who, it so happens, also attended Oak Park High School. This is one of the very few Hemingway works which have been published in an illustrated edition. On November 26, 1941, FOR WHOM THE BELL TOLLS was awarded The Limited Editions Club Gold Medal—"to that American author who is considered to have written the book which most closely approaches the stature of a classic." The committee of award was Clifton Fadiman, Sinclair Lewis and Sterling North.

ACROSS THE RIVER AND INTO THE TREES

was published serially in Cosmopolitan magazine February to June, 1950. The book was published by Scribners on September 7 of the same year. There were 75,000 copies in the first printing. The first twenty-five copies, containing a few errors, might be called the first issue of the first edition.

The Short Stories

INDICATING FIRST APPEARANCE IN
PERIODICALS AND/OR BOOKS

UP IN MICHIGAN

in THREE STORIES AND TEN POEMS.

MY OLD MAN

in THREE STORIES AND TEN POEMS. This story also appeared in Best Short Stories of 1923 edited by Edw. J. O'Brien and published by Small, Maynard & Co., Boston—early in 1924. This was the first publication of a Hemingway story in book form in the United States. Incidentally, the book was dedicated to E. H., but his name was spelled incorrectly as "hemenway."

OUT OF SEASON

in THREE STORIES AND TEN POEMS.

A VERY SHORT STORY

Chapter X—in our time, Paris—1924.

THE REVOLUTIONIST

Chapter XI—in our time, Paris—1924.

L'ENVOI

Chapter XVIII—in our time, Paris—1924.

INDIAN CAMP

first appeared entitled (as Work in Progress) in the Transatlantic Review—April, 1924. In book form in IN OUR TIME.

THE DOCTOR AND THE DOCTOR'S WIFE

in the Transatlantic Review—November, 1924, and in IN OUR TIME.

THE END OF SOMETHING

in IN OUR TIME—New York, 1925.

THE THREE DAY BLOW

in IN OUR TIME—New York, 1925.

THE BATTLER

in IN OUR TIME—New York, 1925.

SOLDIERS HOME

in Contact Collection of Contemporary Writers—Three Mountain Press—Paris, 1925. There were 300 copies. Also in IN OUR TIME.

MR. AND MRS. ELLIOT

in the Little Review—Paris—Juan Gris No. 1924–25. Also in IN OUR TIME.

CAT IN THE RAIN

in IN OUR TIME—New York, 1925.

CROSS COUNTRY SNOW

in Transatlantic Review—December, 1924 and IN OUR TIME, New York, 1925.

BIG TWO HEARTED RIVER

in This Quarter—Paris, May, 1925 and In Our Time, New York, 1925.

THE UNDEFEATED

was originally published in German as "Der Stierkampf" in Der Querschnitt, Frankfort, 1924. Its first appearance in English was in This Quarter—Paris, 1925–26. The first appearance in book form was in The Best Short Stories of 1926—published by Dodd, Mead & Co. in New York, December 4, 1926.

TODAY IS FRIDAY

published separately in 1926 is included in this group as it appeared later in several of the collections of short stories starting with Men Without Women, New York, 1927.

IN ANOTHER COUNTRY

in Scribner's Magazine—New York—April, 1927 and Men Without Women.

HILLS LIKE WHITE ELEPHANTS

in transition—Paris—August, 1927 and Men Without Women.

THE KILLERS

in Scribner's—March, 1927 and Men Without Women. Best Short Stories of 1927 was published at the same time and also contained The Killers.

ITALY—1927

in the New Republic, May 18, 1927. When this story appeared in MEN WITHOUT WOMEN it was retitled CHE TI DICE LA PATRIA.

FIFTY GRAND

in the Atlantic Monthly, July, 1927 and MEN WITHOUT WOMEN.

A SIMPLE ENQUIRY

in MEN WITHOUT WOMEN.

TEN INDIANS

in MEN WITHOUT WOMEN.

A CANARY FOR ONE

in Scribner's, April, 1927 and MEN WITHOUT WOMEN.

AN ALPINE IDYLL

was published in MEN WITHOUT WOMEN and also The American Caravan, A Yearbook of American Literature – The Macauley Co.—New York, 1927.

A PURSUIT RACE

in MEN WITHOUT WOMEN.

BANAL STORY

in the Little Review—Spring Summer 1926 issue; also MEN WITHOUT WOMEN.

NOW I LAY ME

in MEN WITHOUT WOMEN.

AFTER THE STORM

in Cosmopolitan May, 1932 and WINNER TAKE NOTHING.

A CLEAN, WELL-LIGHTED PLACE

in Scribner's Magazine—March, 1933 and WINNER TAKE NOTHING.

THE LIGHT OF THE WORLD

in WINNER TAKE NOTHING.

THE SEA CHANGE

in This Quarter—Paris—December, 1931 and WINNER TAKE NOTHING.

A WAY YOU'LL NEVER BE

in WINNER TAKE NOTHING.

THE MOTHER OF A QUEEN

in WINNER TAKE NOTHING.

ONE READER WRITES

in WINNER TAKE NOTHING.

HOMAGE TO SWITZERLAND

in Scribner's Magazine – April, 1933 and WINNER TAKE NOTHING.

A DAY'S WAIT

in WINNER TAKE NOTHING.

A NATURAL HISTORY OF THE DEAD

in WINNER TAKE NOTHING.

WINE OF WYOMING

in Scribner's Magazine – August, 1930 and WINNER TAKE NOTHING. This was E. H.'s first short story after A FAREWELL TO ARMS.

ON THE QUAI AT SMYRNA

appeared originally as the introduction to the 1930 reissue of IN OUR TIME. When it was published in THE FIFTH COLUMN AND THE FIRST FORTY-NINE STORIES it was given its title.

GOD REST YOU MERRY GENTLEMEN

although one of the short stories, was published separately in book form by the House of Books, New York, 1933.

ONE TRIP ACROSS

in Cosmopolitan, April, 1934 and as Part I of TO HAVE AND HAVE NOT with some changes.

FATHERS AND SONS

in WINNER TAKE NOTHING.

THE TRADESMAN'S RETURN

in Esquire—February, 1936. Subsequently published as Chapters 6, 7 and 8 of TO HAVE AND HAVE NOT with some changes.

THE HORNS OF THE BULL

in Esquire—June, 1936. When this story was published in THE FIFTH COLUMN AND THE FIRST FORTY-NINE STORIES it was retitled THE CAPITAL OF THE WORLD.

GIVE US A PRESCRIPTION, DOCTOR

in Scribner's Magazine—April, 1933 and WINNER TAKE NOTHING, retitled THE GAMBLER THE NUN AND THE RADIO.

OLD MAN AT THE BRIDGE

in Ken—May 9, 1938 and THE FIFTH COLUMN AND THE FIRST FORTY-NINE STORIES.

THE SNOWS OF KILIMANJARO

in Esquire—August, 1936 and THE FIFTH COLUMN AND THE FIRST FORTY-NINE STORIES.

THE SHORT HAPPY LIFE OF FRANCIS MACOMBER

in Cosmopolitan—September, 1936 and THE FIFTH COLUMN AND THE FIRST FORTY-NINE STORIES.

Short Stories

WHICH HAVE NOT AS YET BEEN PUBLISHED IN BOOK FORM

not included in previous group

THE MAN WITH THE TYROLESE HAT

in Der Querschnitt, Frankfort, 1936.

THE DENUNCIATION

in Esquire—November, 1938.

THE BUTTERFLY AND THE TANK

in Esquire—December, 1938.

NIGHT BEFORE BATTLE

in Esquire—February, 1939.

NOBODY EVER DIES

in Cosmopolitan—March, 1939.

UNDER THE RIDGE

in Cosmopolitan—October, 1939.

Poetry

THEY ALL MADE PEACE, WHAT IS PEACE

was originally published in the Little Review, Paris, Spring, 1923. It appeared in Poetry, A Magazine of Verse, Chicago, February, 1931 and in book form in the Active Anthology, edited by Ezra Pound and published by Faber and Faber, Ltd., London, October, 1933.

ULTIMATELY

In June, 1922 this poem appeared in a magazine called the Double Dealer. It was published in New Orleans. Salamagundi by William Faulkner was published in June, 1932 by the Casanova Press, Milwaukee. There were 525 copies printed and ULTIMATELY was on the back cover.

WANDERINGS

This title covered the following six poems which appeared for the first time in Poetry, A Magazine of Verse – Chicago – January, 1923:

MITRAILIATRICE
OILY WEATHER
ROOSEVELT
RIPARTO D'ASSALTO
CHAMPS D'HONNEUR
CHAPTER HEADING

THREE STORIES–TEN POEMS

Published in Paris in 1923 contains four new poems in addition to the six previously published in Poetry, A Magazine of Verse

OKLAHOMA
MONTPARNASSE
ALONG WITH YOUTH
CAPTIVES

THE EARNEST LIBERALS LAMENT

in Der Querschnitt–Frankfort–Autumn, 1924.

THE SOUL OF SPAIN WITH
McALMON AND BIRD THE PUBLISHERS (PART 1)

in Der Querschnitt–Frankfort–Autumn, 1924.

THE SOUL OF SPAIN WITH
McALMON AND BIRD THE PUBLISHERS (PART 2)

in Der Querschnitt–Frankfort–November, 1924.

THE LADY POETS WITH FOOTNOTES

in Der Querschnitt–Frankfort–November, 1924.

THE AGE DEMANDED

in Der Querschnitt–Frankfort–February, 1925.

NOTHOEMIST POEM

The name of this poem was spelled incorrectly when it appeared in an anthology entitled Exiles, edited by Ezra Pound and published in Paris in the spring of 1927. Back to Montparnasse by Sisley Huddleston was published in Philadelphia in 1931 by J. B. Lippincott & Co., and contained a reprinting of NEOTHOMIST POEM, spelled correctly.

VALENTINE

in the Little Review, Paris, 1929.

Contributions to Periodicals

(OTHER THAN STORIES)

AND TO THE UNITED STATES

Transatlantic Review, May, 1924.

AND FROM THE UNITED STATES

Transatlantic Review. This issue was edited by E. H.

PAMPLOMA LETTER

Transatlantic Review, September, 1924.

CONRAD, OPTIMIST AND MORALIST

Transatlantic Review, September, 1924.

HOMAGE TO EZRA

This Quarter, Paris, May, 1925.

MY OWN LIFE

The New Yorker, February 12, 1927.

BULLFIGHTING, SPORT AND INDUSTRY

Fortune, March, 1930. This article was illustrated with reproductions of Goya, Manet and Zuloaga.

MARLIN OFF THE MORRO

A Cuban letter–Esquire, Autumn, 1933.

THE FRIEND OF SPAIN

A Spanish letter–Esquire, January, 1934.

A PARIS LETTER

Esquire, February, 1934.

a.d. IN AFRICA

A Tanganyika Letter—Esquire, April, 1934.

SHOOTISM VERSUS SPORT

The Second Tanganyika Letter—Esquire, June, 1934.

NOTES ON DANGEROUS GAME

The Third Tanganyika Letter, Esquire, July, 1934.

OUT IN THE STREAM

A Cuban Letter—Esquire, August, 1934.

DEFENSE OF DIRTY WORDS

A Cuban Letter—Esquire, September, 1934.

GENIO AFTER JOSIE

A Havana Letter—Esquire, October, 1934.

OLD NEWSMAN WRITES

A letter from Cuba—Esquire, December, 1934.

NOTES ON LIFE AND LETTERS

or a manuscript found in a bottle, Esquire, January, 1935.

REMEMBERING SHOOTING—FLYING

A Key West Letter—Esquire, February, 1935.

SAILFISH OFF MOMBASA

A Key West Letter—Esquire, March, 1935.

THE SIGHTS OF WHITEHEAD STREET

A Key West Letter—Esquire, April, 1935.

a.d. SOUTHERN STYLE

A Key West Letter—Esquire, May, 1935.

ON BEING SHOT AGAIN

A Gulf Stream Letter—Esquire, June, 1935.

THE PRESIDENT VANQUISHES

A Bimini Letter—Esquire, July, 1935.

HE WHO GETS SLAP HAPPY

A Bimini Letter—Esquire, August, 1935.

NOTES ON THE NEXT WAR

A serious topical letter—Esquire, September, 1935.

MONOLOGUE TO THE MAESTRO

A High Seas Letter—Esquire, October, 1935.

THE MALADY OF POWER

A Second Serious Letter—Esquire, November, 1935.

MILLION DOLLAR FRIGHT

A New York Letter—Esquire, December, 1935.

WINGS ALWAYS OVER AFRICA

An ornithological letter—Esquire, January, 1936.

ON THE BLUE WATER

A Gulf Stream Letter—Esquire, April, 1936.

THERE SHE BREACHES

or Moby Dick off the Morro—Esquire, May, 1936.

GATTORNO—PROGRAM NOTE

Esquire, May, 1936.

THE MAN WITH THE TYROLESE HAT

Der Querschnitt, June, 1936.

ON THE MADRID FRONT

Hemingway Reports Spain—The New Republic, May 5, 1937.

HEMINGWAY REPORTS SPAIN

The New Republic, January 12, 1938.

THE TIME NOW, THE PLACE SPAIN

Ken—April 7, 1938.

DYING, WELL OR BADLY

Ken—April 21, 1938.

REPORT FROM SPAIN

Hemingway Reports Spain—The New Republic, April 27, 1938.

THE HEAT AND THE COLD

Remembering Turning the Spanish Earth—the Ivens, Hemingway film of the Spanish war—Verve, Paris, spring, 1938.

THE CARDINAL PICKS A WINNER

Ken, May 5, 1938.

UNITED WE FALL UPON KEN

Ken—June 2, 1938.

REPORT FROM SPAIN

Hemingway Reports Spain—The New Republic, June 8, 1938.

H.M.'S LOYAL STATE DEPARTMENT

Ken—June 16, 1938.

TREACHERY IN ARAGON

Ken—June 30, 1938.

CALL FOR GREATNESS

Ken—July 14, 1938.

THE SPANISH WAR

fact, a magazine published in London, devoted its July, 1938 issue to five articles by E. H. They were:

THE SAVING OF MADRID (On the Guadalajara Front—March 23, 1937).
THE ARAGON FRONT (On the Aragon Front—September 14, 1937).
TERUEL (Army Headquarters, Teruel Front—December 20, 1937).
FRANCO ADVANCING (Barcelona—April 3, 1938).
LAST DESPATCHES (Castellon—May 9, 1938).

MY PAL THE GORILLA GARGANTUA

Ken—July 28, 1938.

A PROGRAM FOR U. S. REALISM

Ken—August 11, 1938.

GOOD GENERALS HUG THE LINE

Ken—August 25, 1938.

FALSE NEWS TO THE PRESIDENT

Ken—September 8, 1938.

FRESH AIR ON AN INSIDE STORY

Ken—September 22, 1938.

THE NEXT OUTBREAK OF PEACE

Ken—January 12, 1939.

THE CLARK'S FORK VALLEY—WYOMING

Vogue, Americana Number—February 1, 1939.

ON THE AMERICAN DEAD IN SPAIN

The New Masses—Lincoln Brigade Number—February 14, 1939. This issue also carried a picture of E. H. and a short comment.

VOYAGE TO VICTORY

Colliers—July 22, 1944.

LONDON FIGHTS THE ROBOTS

Colliers—August 19, 1944.

BATTLE FOR PARIS

Colliers—September 30, 1944.

HOW WE CAME TO PARIS

Colliers—October 7, 1944.

THE G.I. AND THE GENERAL

Colliers—November 4, 1944.

WAR IN THE SIEGFRIED LINE

Colliers—November 18, 1944.

THE GREAT BLUE RIVER

Holiday—July, 1949.

THE GOOD LION
THE FAITHFUL BULL

These two fables appeared in Holiday magazine, in the March, 1951 issue. They were illustrated by Adriana Ivancich.

First Appearance

IN BOOK FORM

OF SOME OF THE PRECEDING ARTICLES

MY OWN LIFE

subtitled "After Reading the Second Volume of Frank Harris' MY LIFE"—in New Yorker Scrap Book—Doubleday Doran—New York, 1931.

NOTES ON THE NEXT WAR

in the Third New Year—Esquire, Inc.—Chicago—New York—1935. The edition was limited to 500 copies.

THE MALADY OF POWER

in American Points of View—A Readers Guide 1936—edited by William H. Cordell and Kathryn Coe Cordell—published by Doubleday Doran—New York, 1937.

ON THE BLUE WATER

in Blow the Man Down—edited by Eric Devine and published by Doubleday Doran—New York, 1937.

THE CLARKS FORK VALLEY, WYOMING

in Vogue's First Reader—published by Julian Messner, Inc.—New York, 1942.

THE LOYALISTS

in They Were There—edited by Curt Riess and published by G. P. Putnam's Sons—New York, 1944. The Loyalists appeared originally as a despatch to the N.A.N.A.

REMEMBERING SHOOTING–FLYING

in Esquire's First Sports Reader–edited by Herbert Graffis and published by A. S. Barnes & Co.–New York, 1945.

HOMAGE TO EZRA

in An Examination of Ezra Pound–a collection of essays–edited by Peter Russell and published by New Directions–New York, November, 1950.

Prefaces and Introductions

KIKI'S MEMOIRS

Translated from the French by Samuel Putnam. Published by Edward W. Titus—At the Sign of the Black Manikin Press—Paris, 1930. Introduction by E. H.

INTRODUCTION TO "KIKI OF MONTPARNASSE"

published in New York in 1929 by Edward W. Titus. There were twenty-five copies printed, apparently to protect the copyright. The pamphlet was dated 1929 but copyrighted in 1930.

THE GREAT CRUSADE

By Gustave Regler. Published by Longmans, Green & Co.—New York, 1940. Preface by E. H., Camaguey, Cuba, 1940. The preface was originally published alone, about three months before the publication of the book.

MEN AT WAR

"The Best War Stories of All Time" was published in 1942 by Crown Publishers, N. Y. It was edited by E. H., who also wrote the introduction and included a very short editor's note. Apparently the only material of his own which E. H. cared to include was: THE CHAUFFEURS OF MADRID, THE FIGHT ON THE HILLTOP, from FOR WHOM THE BELL TOLLS and THE RETREAT FROM CAPORETTO from A FAREWELL TO ARMS.

THE EDUCATION OF A FRENCH MODEL

This book, published by Boar's Head Books, New York, 1950, is a reprint of the Paris, 1930 edition. Many new photographs have been added to this edition but E. H.'s introduction is unchanged. It is believed that this book was published without E. H.'s O.K.

As Hemingway's work has been widely used in anthologies

and other types of collections

no attempt will be made herein to list such items

The following brief note indicates those few articles

which have appeared only once and as indicated

MEN IN THE RANKS

"The Story of 12 Americans in Spain" by Joseph North. Published by Friends of the Abraham Lincoln Brigade —New York, March, 1939. Foreword by E. H.

TREASURY FOR THE FREE WORLD

Edited by Ben Raeburn and published by the Arco Publishing Co., New York, February, 1946. Foreword by E. H., San Francisco de Paula, Cuba, September, 1945. The foreword appeared as THE SLING AND THE PEBBLE in Free World, An International Magazine for the United Nations, March, 1946.

THIS MUST BE THE PLACE

Memoirs of Montparnasse. By James Charters (Jimmie the Barman), published by Herbert Joseph, Ltd.—London—1934. Introduction by E. H., Serengetti Plains, Tanganyika, December, 1934.

ALL GOOD AMERICANS

By Jerome Bahr. Published by Charles Scribner's Sons —New York, 1937. Preface by E. H.

ALL THE BRAVE

"Drawings of the Spanish War" by Louis Quintanilla. Text by Elliot Paul and Jay Allen. Published by Modern Age Books—New York, 1939. The preface by E. H. contained three sections indicated respectively, March

10, 1938, Key West–April 18, 1938, Somewhere in Spain–May, 1938, Somewhere in Spain. A limited (to 450 copies) numbered edition, signed by Quintanilla, was published simultaneously with the trade edition.

ATLANTIC GAME FISHING

By S. Kip Farrington, Jr. Published by the Garden City Publishing Co., New York, 1939. Introduction by E. H.

STUDIO EUROPE

By John Groth. Published by Vanguard Press, New York, 1945. Introduction by E. H., August 25, 1945, San Francisco de Paula.

IN SICILY

by Elio Vittorini was published by New Directions, New York, 1949. E. H. wrote the introduction in Cortina D'Ampezzo.

MARLIN OFF CUBA

in American Big Game Fishing published by Hutchinson & Co., London, for the Derrydale Press, New York, 1935. There were 950 copies of this book.

THE LOYALISTS

in They Were There by Curt Riess–Published by G. P. Putnam's Sons–New York, 1944.

CUBAN FISHING

in Game Fish of the World, published by Harper & Bros., New York, 1949, edited by Brian Vesey and Francesca La Monte.

THE WRITER AND WAR

in The Writer in a Changing World—Copyright by The League of American Authors—Equinox Corp. Press—New York, 1937.

THE CHAUFFEURS OF MADRID

was a despatch to the N.A.N.A. and later appeared in Men at War, New York, 1942.

Unclassified Work

HOW BALLAD WRITING AFFECTS OUR SENIORS

This article appeared in the Tabula, an Oak Park High School, Ill. (at which E. H. was a student) publication in November, 1916.

SEPI JINGAN

appeared in the same publication, in the same issue.

THE WORKER

was published in the Tabula, March, 1917.

CLASS PROPHECY

E. H. wrote his class prophecy for the June, 1917 issue of Tabula. The full name of the high school referred to above is the Oak Park and River Township High School.

A DIVINE GESTURE

was published in the Double Dealer, a magazine, New Orleans, May, 1922.

A LETTER

An extract from a letter which appeared in Scribner's Magazine, March, 1927. This was the issue which contained THE KILLERS, which was the first story by E. H. in an American magazine.

THE REAL SPANIARD

This article was in The Boulevardier, a magazine published in Paris, October, 1927. Although E. H. undoubtedly wrote the piece originally, it was so rewritten by the editor as to be unrecognizable as Hemingway's work.

WHO KNOWS HOW?

Harcourt, Brace & Co., New York, published Creating the Short Story in 1929. It was a symposium anthology by Henry Goodman and contained E. H.'s WHO KNOWS HOW?.

EXCERPTS FROM LETTER

In October, 1930, the Walden Book Shop of Chicago issued a paper containing some biographical notes on E. H. and some excerpts from a letter written by him.

BASTARD NOTE

The p. (x) proof sheet from the first edition, second issue, of A Farewell to Arms was reprinted in facsimile, with a humorous comment by E. H. The run consisted of 97 copies—the date, 1931.

LUIS QUINTANILLA

The catalogue for an exhibition of paintings by Quintanilla (Pierre Matisse Gallery) contained a long article by E. H. The catalogue was dated November 20 to December 4 (1934), New York. The article was reprinted (with minor changes) in Esquire, February, 1935.

JOAN MIRO

Leaflet containing first appearance of part of an article on Joan Miro–New York, 1934. The complete article appeared in Cahier's D'Art.

GATTORNO

E. H. wrote a long comment and biographical sketch on Antonio Gattorno. This was contained in an Havana, April, 1935 publication devoted to thirty-eight reproductions of this Cuban painter's work. Critical opinions by John Dos Passos, Ramon Guirao, Alejo Carpentier, and E. Aviles Raminez were included. There were 460 copies of the book. This article was reprinted along with reproductions of some of Gattorno's paintings in Esquire, May, 1936.

SO RED THE NOSE

was published by Farrar & Rinehart, December, 1935, New York. It is a booklet containing cocktail recipes by various authors and includes E. H.'s Death in the Afternoon cocktail and a short comment by him.

PORTRAITS AND SELF PORTRAITS

By Georges Schreiber, Houghton Mifflin, Boston, 1936, contains a short autobiographical article by E. H. written in Key West.

TWO WARS AND MORE TO COME

A facsimile of a cablegram (January 10, 1938) from E. H. to the publishers of Herbert Matthews' "Two Wars and More to Come" was used as advertising material in connection with the sale of the book.

WRITERS TAKE SIDE

published by the League of American Authors, New York, May, 1938, is a collection of letters about the war in Spain from 418 American authors. There is a very brief comment on the subject by E. H.

SPANISH PORTRAITS

by Jo Davidson, is a group of pictures of his sculptures of various people who were in the Spanish war. Each picture is accompanied by a comment on the subject by some well known author. E. H. wrote a comment on Milton Wolf. The book was published in New York by the Georgian Press in 1939.

THIS IS MY BEST

published by the Deal Press, New York, 1942 and edited by Whit Burnett, is a collection of selections by American authors of their best work and the reasons for their selections. E. H. "suggested" the reprinting of THE SHORT AND HAPPY LIFE OF FRANCIS MACOMBER with the comment that it was as "reprintable" as any other of his stories.

GREETINGS

to the Cincinnati Symphony Orchestra on the occasion of their Golden Jubilee, was contained in their program, March 23 and 24, 1945.

JOAN MIRO

by Clement Greenberg, was published by the Quadrangle Press, New York, 1948. It contains the complete article, part of which originally appeared in a leaflet in 1934.

LETTERS

The New Colophon, A Book–Collector's Miscellany, New York, 1950, contains excerpts from several letters from E. H. to Gertrude Stein.

IMPORTANT AUTHORS OF THE FALL SPEAKING FOR THEMSELVES

appeared in the New York Herald Tribune Book Review on October 8th, 1950 and contained a contribution by E. H.

SUCCESS, IT'S WONDERFUL

by Harvey Breit, appeared in the New York Times Book Review on December 3rd, 1950. The title is Mr. Breit's. E. H.'s contribution to this article consists of his reply to a question asked of the writers of some of the best selling novels of 1950. The query sought to find out how the writers of best sellers reacted to their success, whether their lives and plans were altered, whether they thought best-seller writers hold certain qualities in common, etc., etc.

LETTERS

The Far Side of Paradise, by Arthur Mizener, published by Houghton Mifflin Co., Boston, January, 1951, contains a number of letters from E. H. to F. Scott Fitzgerald.